SUPERBIKE
2007/2008

Superbike Welcome

Summary

That's Superbike	6
James Toseland	12
Superbike Riders	22
Honda Ten Take	30
Yamaha Motor Italia	40
Ducati Xerox Team	50
Suzuki Alstare Corona Extra	60
Kawasaki PSG-1 Corse	70
Superbike Races	80
Kenan Sofouglu	110
Supersport Riders	116
Supersport Races	122
Superstock 1000	140
Superstock 600	154
History	165
The best	222

Published by
EditVALLARDI per conto FGSport- Roma-Italy
© 2007 EditVALLARDI
Via Roma,74 - 20060 Cassina de Pecchi (MI) - Italy
Tel (+39) 02 95 28 202 - Fax (+39) 02 95 29 9446
Email : segreteria@editvallardi.com

Concept
Claudio Porrozzi

Photo Editor
Fabrizio Porrozzi

Art Editor
Cinzia Giuriolo

Photographers
Fabrizio Porrozzi
Alessandro Piredda
Grame Brown

Texts
Claudio Porrozzi
Luca Sordi
Federico Porrozzi

Graphics
Alessandro Petrangeli

Printed by
Poligrafica ANTENORE srl - Padova - Italy

Cover by
Zanardi Group srl - Padova - Italy

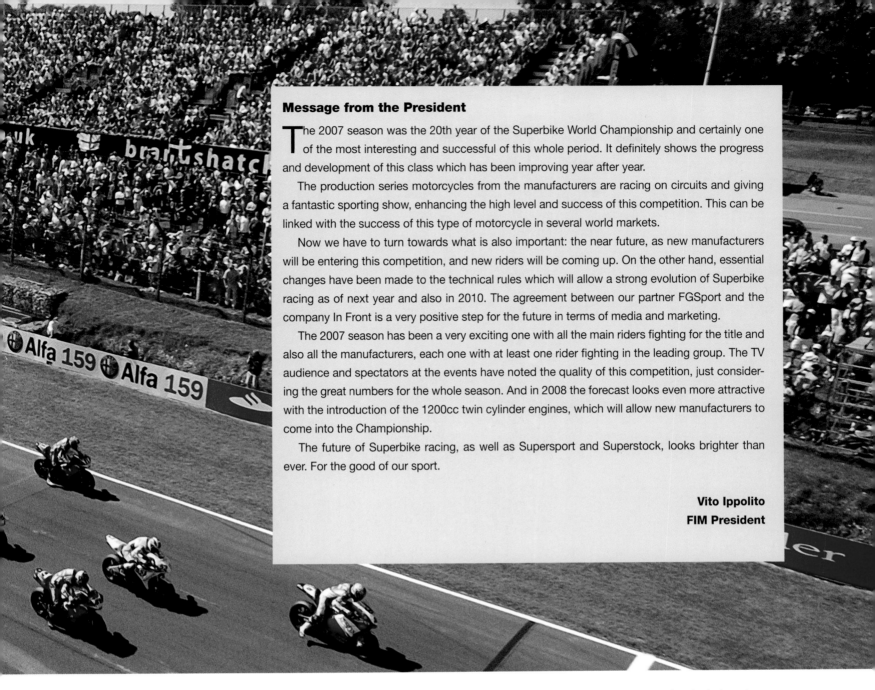

Message from the President

The 2007 season was the 20th year of the Superbike World Championship and certainly one of the most interesting and successful of this whole period. It definitely shows the progress and development of this class which has been improving year after year.

The production series motorcycles from the manufacturers are racing on circuits and giving a fantastic sporting show, enhancing the high level and success of this competition. This can be linked with the success of this type of motorcycle in several world markets.

Now we have to turn towards what is also important: the near future, as new manufacturers will be entering this competition, and new riders will be coming up. On the other hand, essential changes have been made to the technical rules which will allow a strong evolution of Superbike racing as of next year and also in 2010. The agreement between our partner FGSport and the company In Front is a very positive step for the future in terms of media and marketing.

The 2007 season has been a very exciting one with all the main riders fighting for the title and also all the manufacturers, each one with at least one rider fighting in the leading group. The TV audience and spectators at the events have noted the quality of this competition, just considering the great numbers for the whole season. And in 2008 the forecast looks even more attractive with the introduction of the 1200cc twin cylinder engines, which will allow new manufacturers to come into the Championship.

The future of Superbike racing, as well as Supersport and Superstock, looks brighter than ever. For the good of our sport.

Vito Ippolito
FIM President

The World Superbike Championship reaches 20 years of age.

As always happens, whenever one is faced with a watershed the mind tends to analyse the past and the present, draw up a balance-sheet and imagine the future.

If we look back on the path we have taken and remember all the anxieties, the efforts and the problems encountered and overcome throughout this twenty-year period, we can only be proud of the results achieved.

In short, the World Superbike Championship represents the only new category in post-war motor sport to have become firmly established on a world level and to have carved out a place for itself alongside Formula 1 and Grand Prix Road Racing.

This result is undoubtedly due to a formula with a winning DNA, but also and above all to a passion that has pervaded every single one of the protagonists of our championship right from the very start.

From all the people who work in our company, to the teams, the representatives of the media who have always believed in our venture, to the commercial and business partners who have in different ways contributed to the growth of the World Superbike Championship and last, but not least, to the International Motorcycling Federation with whom we are honoured to have been an institutional partner for almost thirty years.

These entities and the passion of the people who belong to them have given rise to an unstoppable force which in a relatively short period of time has helped to turn what was a series mainly for amateurs into one of the biggest and most exciting forms of motor sport on the planet.

Sport however teaches us to look forwards rather than backwards and to never consider entirely satisfactory the objectives reached.

Our commitment and our undivided attention are therefore totally orientated towards the future.

The World Superbike Championship is gearing up for a further period of growth that already in the next three years will drastically increase participation levels due to the arrival of major new manufacturers and teams, and as a result its popularity, media presence and appeal will also all grow.

Dear friends and fans, all of us here in FGSport are ready to give you a fantastic show and adrenaline for another twenty years. So warm up your engines, the lights are about to go green for a new start!

Maurizio and Paolo Flammini

That's Superbike

There's a good atmosphere in Superbike. It is one of the key aspects of a category that has numerous points in its favour which help to make it a great place to be in the world of professional motorcycle racing.

It is a formula for true fans, who are competent and above all experts at picking up all the ideas and indications that come from the track and the paddock. This sparks off a series of debates that help to boost interest in Superbike which, as spectator figures show, is constantly on the increase.

Another key aspect of the world championship for bikes derived from road-going models is the riders themselves. Apart from a few exceptions, they are riders who love to experience the paddock, meet their rivals off the track and above all, they are always at the disposal of their fans and supporters in general. With these guys around, it is impossible not to like Superbike!

Just as it is also impossible not to admire the beautiful girls who are always present in the paddock and on the world championship grid: hostesses, umbrella girls, but also riders' wives and girlfriends who all help to render the environment brighter and better (always assuming it is necessary!)

That's Superbike!

That's Superbike

That's Superbike

PIST⬤L RACING ®

Ten Kate
HONDA
CBR 1000RR

2007 SUPERBIKE
World Champion

The natural piston choice for winners ...

... also used by:

PSG-1 KAWASAKI / **DFX** HONDA

Pedercini DUCATI / **Alto Evolution** HONDA

MG Competition YAMAHA France *YEC...*

Pistal Racing S.r.l.- Via N. Sardi,82/B - 14030 Rocchetta Tanaro - (AT) - ITALY
☎+39.0141.644816 - 🖷 +39.0141.644970
commerciale@pistalracing.it - www.pistalracing.it

SUPERBIKE
Champion

James Toseland

Toseland was certainly one of the favourites for victory in 2007 but there were a number of other top riders on the list as well to compete for the twentieth World Superbike title.

After several seasons on a Ducati, including 2004 when he won his first world title, the British rider lined up for his second season on a Honda CBR1000RR with the Dutch Ten Kate Honda outfit. He had already come close to his second title in 2006, when he finished runner-up on the Winston-sponsored machine, but this year on the Hanspree bike he showed greater determination to win the Riders' title, despite committing a number of errors.

Despite his relatively young age, Tose-

land has already had a long career in racing. Born on October 5th in Sheffield, after gaining experience in trials and minor formulas he made his debut in the 1997 British Supersport championship, finishing third overall.

The following year 'JT' made the leap up to world championship level with a factory Honda in Supersport. It was a traumatic experience for the 18-year-old and James could only finish 18th overall, improving to 11th the following year. He made a wise decision to move back home to take part in the British Superbike championship, and then returned to the world scene in 2001.

Ducati GSE offered him their twin-cylin-

James Toseland

James Toseland

der machine and James eased his way into the world championship, improving year after year. He struck gold in 2004 when he won the world title against all odds, defeating his team-mate Regis Laconi at the final round.

In 2005 he was unable to repeat his title-winning performance and was replaced by Ducati the following year. Toseland was left with little else but to move to the Honda Ten Kate team and the rest is recent history.

The 2007 season began with five wins in 12 races and a lead of 35 points over his

James Toseland

closest rivals. He then failed to get on the podium at Silverstone and Misano and his lead was gradually being whittled down. James put things right again with a victory at Brno and a fantastic double win at Brands Hatch in front of his home crowd, which increased his lead to 66 points over Haga, a gap that looked comfortable enough for him to wrap up the title.

But things took a turn for the worse in the final three rounds with a crash at Vallelunga, just like Silverstone, and James came to the final race at Magny-Cours in crisis, with a 29 point lead over two riders of the calibre of Biaggi and Haga. After race 1 his lead over Haga had been cut to just 17 points, but in race 2 team-mate Rolfo watched his back and Toseland managed to maintain a tight margin of just two points over his Japanese rival.

There are probably many reasons for the end-of-season crisis but probably the biggest one was his decision to move to MotoGP. Toseland leaves Superbike after 166 races, in which he obtained 57 podiums and 16 wins.

James Toseland

SUPERBIKE
Riders

A championship that concludes after 25 races with the top 2 riders separated by a couple of points (and the top 3 separated by 18) is a sure sign of competitive racing. James Toseland never abandoned the top slot throughout the year but several riders took turns in the positions behind him. One of them was Max Biaggi, who catalyzed the attention of the media and the public before, during and after the actual running of the championship. Sometimes it seemed that Superbike revolved around the Italian, which certainly helped to increase the rivalry between him and the other riders, but let's have a look at the situation behind the winner.

Toseland, who fully deserved his second title, was followed home by Noriyuki Haga, who certainly deserved to win his first this year. The 32-year-old Japanese rider had a flawless run throughout the season, and his only DNFs were at Assen with a technical problem and Misano, where he made 'contact' with Biaggi. The rest of

Noriyuki Haga

Troy Corser

Max Biaggi

Troy Bayliss

the Yamaha rider's season was perfect, and he stepped onto the podium 15 times, just missing out on the title for the third time by two points.

Max Biaggi probably thought he could win the title at the first attempt. At the age of 35, he accepted the World Superbike challenge for Suzuki and began the season well with a win and a second place at the opening round in Qatar. The Roman was then almost never off the podium for the rest of the year, and he added two more wins at Brno and Vallelunga to his total. In the end the 'Pirate' was still in the title race until the final round and only Toseland (unintentionally) prevented him from being a contender right until the wire at Magny-Cours. In any case, Biaggi's performance in his rookie Superbike season fully lived up to his class, experience and reputation.

Troy Bayliss has already won a couple of World Superbike titles (in 2001 and 2006) but he desperately wanted to win a third one this year. He also really wanted to beat Max Biaggi with whom he shares a healthy rivalry, having also been up against him in MotoGP. Every time his elderly but still competitive Ducati 999 allowed him to, the 38-year-old Australian grasped the opportunity to win races. He did so seven times this year, including a superb double win at Misano which took him to within striking distance of Toseland; then he stumbled a couple of times at Brno and Brands Hatch, losing ground at the top and he eventually finished the season in fourth place.

Another Australian who has been around for some time now, 35-year-old Troy Corser, took his Yamaha to fifth place in 2007 without winning a race. 'Mr Superpole', who has taken forty pole positions in his career, more than any other Superbike rider, probably suffered from being Haga's team-mate this year but when doubts

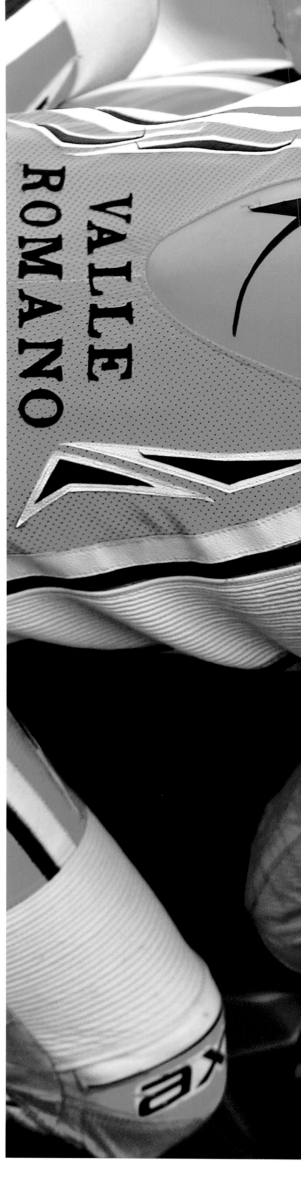

started to emerge about him remaining he put in a series of good performances that led him to be confirmed in the Monza-based Japanese team.

Ruben Xaus was an outsider in the battle for the championship but was always up there at the front. The Spanish rider, on a Sterilgarda Ducati, at least had the satisfaction of finishing ahead of the factory's Lorenzo Lanzi and, in particular, of winning race 1 at Valencia. Ruben is a very popular figure in the paddock and at 29 years of age appears to have found a niche in life that allows him to express himself in the best possible way out on the track. Next up was Lorenzo Lanzi, who performed well below expectations and not to the best of his ability on the second factory Ducati 999. He finished ahead of another Italian in the final standings, Roberto Rolfo on the second Ten Kate Honda CBR. The 27-year-old from Turin put in some good performances in his first

year in Superbike. Another Italian, Michel Fabrizio, paid the price for an uncompetitive DFX Honda CBR and a certain lack of concentration; he only showed what he could do in the races at Brno and Brands Hatch.

The only representative from Germany was Max Neukirchner, who at 23 years of age, came into the Alstare Suzuki team's orbit. He even replaced Kagayama on the factory bike in France, and returned the favour with a positive fourth place.

Regis Laconi and Fonsi Nieto were the only two riders for Kawasaki, which finally boosted its presence in the World Superbike Championship. The PSG-1 team put a major effort into the programme and the two riders used their experience to stay with the front-runners on occasions, but with the exception of Nieto's pole at Lausitz and his third place at Magny-Cours, the results were disappointing.

Fonsi Nieto

HONDA

TEN KATE

This Dutch squad made its debut in Supersport at the end of the 1990s and since 2002 has notched up a long series of championship victories in the feeder category to Superbike with several expert riders but also young talent such as Chris Vermeulen. In 2004 with the new regulations that allowed 1000 cc powered machines to take part in Superbike, the team run by the Ten Kate family made its debut in the top category. The rider chosen for the job was Vermeulen and the team's success has continued since then, with Toseland picking up the title win this year. Despite being directly responsible to Honda Europe, Ten Kate develops a lot of material themselves and is

therefore also a point of reference for the Japanese manufacturer. In the racing department they prepare engines that are then sold to numerous teams in Supersport and, more recently, in Superbike. They also have close contacts with a number of technical partners such as suspension firms.

Honda Ten Kate

HONDA TEN KATE TEAM 2007	
Riders	James Toseland (# 52)
	Roberto Rolfo (# 44)
Team Owner	Gerry Ten Kate
Team Manager	Ronald Ten Kate
Electronics Technician	Norbert Burink
Suspension Technician	Pietre Breddels
Tyre Technician	Jan Thijs
Engineer	Fritz Jaspers
Engineer	Hans Nooter
Press Officer	Beth Robinson
Toseland Crew	
Chief Mechanic	Kor Veldman
Mechanic	William Huisjes
Mechanic	Chris Dudink
Rolfo Crew	
Chief Mechanic	Danny van Erven
Mechanic	Arjan Dekker
Mechanic	Gerrit Tuenter
Team Coordinator	Monique Muggen
Hospitality	Henk Muggen
Hospitality	Janny Muggen

Honda Ten Kate

HONDA CBR 1000 RR FIREBLADE 2007	
Engine	
Type:	four-cylinder, in-line
Displacement:	998 cc
Bore x stroke:	75 x 56,5 mm
Valves:	four per cylinder
Power:	170 hp @ 11,250 rpm
Chassis	
Front suspension:	inverted forks
Rear suspension:	single shock
Trasmission	
Gears:	six-speed
Clutch:	wet, multiplate
Brakes	
Front:	2 x 320 mm floating discs
Rear:	220 mm single disc
Dimensions	
Length:	2.030 mm
Width:	720 mm
Dry weight:	176 Kg.
Wheelbase:	1410 mm
Fuel capacity:	18 litres

Yamaha Motor Italia

After various experiences in the past with British teams and the Valli brothers (Yamaha dealers), Yamaha's Italian subsidiary entered the scene directly in the early 1990s, first with Byrd and then as Yamaha Motor Italia. The squad based at Gerno di Lesmo near Lecco soon became a cornerstone of the Japanese manufacturer's involvement in Superbike, beating off the competition from other European subsidiaries. Victory in the Manufacturers' championship in 2007, as well as the runner-up slot in the Riders' championship, is just reward for the efforts of the Italian squad. It goes without saying that Yamaha Motor Italia, which has an advanced racing department close to the team Headquarters, is present in the world championship with one of the most professional teams around as well as a very popular hospitality unit.

Yamaha Motor Italia

YAMAHA MOTOR ITALIA WSB TEAM 2007	
Riders	Troy Corser (# 11)
	Noriyuki Haga (# 41)
Racing Manager	Claudio Consonni
Team Co-ordinator	Massimo Meregalli
Technical Director	Silvano Galbusera
Chief Engineer	Mauro Saleppicco
Electronics Technician	Marco Venturi
Press Officer	Chiara Pozzi
Haga Crew	
Chief Mechanic	Silvano Galbusera
Electronics Technician	Giulio Nava
Mechanic	Marco Meregalli
Mechanic	Maurizio Mazzolini
Mechanic	Satoshi Ishii
Assistant Mechanic	Alessandro Abbrandini
Corser Crew	
Chief Mechanic	Dave Marton
Electronics Technician	Davide Gentile
Mechanic	Fabrizio Malaguti
Mechanic	Giuliano Poletti
Mechanic	Jurij Pellegrini
Assistant Mechanic	Efisio Putzolu
Hospitality	Karol Teruzzi

Yamaha Motor Italia

YAMAHA YZF-R1 2007	
Engine	
Type:	four-cylinder, in-line
Displacement:	998 cc
Bore x stroke:	77 x 53,6 mm
Chassis	
Frame:	aluminium Deltabox
Front suspension:	Ohlins inverted forks
Rear suspension:	Ohlins single shock
Trasmission	
Gears:	six
Clutch:	wet, multiple disc
Brakes	
Front:	320 mm dual discs
Rear:	203 mm single disc
Dimensions	
Length:	n/a
Width:	n/a
Dry weight:	165 Kg.
Wheelbase:	1415 mm
Fuel capacity:	23 litres

Ducati Xerox Team

Ducati has always supported Superbike and a factory team has been present in the world championship since the early days. The Bologna manufacturer has literally dominated the scene, winning a total of 12 Riders' and 14 Manufacturers' titles. The wins have always been with a twin-cylinder bike, first with the 851 and ending with the 999, which will soon be replaced by the 1098. The list of riders who have raced and won with the red Italian bikes is a long one and includes Marco Lucchinelli, Raymond Roche, Doug Polen, Carl Fogarty, Troy Corser, Troy Bayliss, Neil Hodgson and James Toseland, all of whom (with the exception of 'Lucky') became world champi-

ons. A number of ex-racers have also been in charge of the factory team, starting with Marco Lucchinelli, continuing with Virginio Ferrari and ending up with Davide Tardozzi who has held this position since 1999. In the past the Superbike team has also been flanked by a Supersport outfit, and is now supported by a Superstock squad. One of the cornerstones in the paddock is the Italian manufacturer's hospitality unit, which gives food and drink to the riders, team members, guests and sponsors but is also a place of pilgrimage for fans from all over the world.

Ducati Xerox Team

DUCATI XEROX TEAM 2007	
Riders	Troy Bayliss (# 21)
	Lorenzo Lanzi (# 57)
Team Manager	Davide Tardozzi
Technical Director	Ernesto Marinelli
Chief Engineer	Karl Putz
Engineer	Francisco Prieto
Press Officer	Julian Thomas
Bayliss Crew	
Track Engineer	Ernesto Marinelli
Electronics Engineer	Alessandra Balducci
Chief Mechanic	Alberto Colombo
Mechanic	Roberto Banci
Mechanic	Fabrizio Longhini
Mechanic	Stefano Favalini
Assistant Mechanic	Moris Grassi
Lanzi Crew	
Track Engineer	Massimo Bartolini
Electronics Engineer	Luca Minelli
Chief Mechanic	Marco Ventura
Mechanic	Andrea Neri
Mechanic	Claudio Montanari
Mechanic	Davide Gibertini
Assistant Mechanic	Leonardo Gena
Storeman	Lindo Sbaraglia
Hospitality	Claudia Guenzani
Logistics	Manuela Barbieri

DUCATI 999R FACTORY 2007	
Engine	
Type:	Twin-cylinder, L-shaped, 90°
Displacement:	999 cc
Bore x stroke:	104 x 58.8 mm
Valves:	four per cylinder
Power:	194 hp @ 12500 rpm
Chassis	
Frame:	tubular steel trellis
Front suspension:	Ohlins upside-down forks
Rear suspension:	Ohlins single shock
Transmission	
Gears:	six-speed
Clutch:	dry
Brakes	
Make:	Brembo
Front:	2 x 290 or 320 mm floating discs
Rear:	1 x 218mm floating disc
Dimensions	
Length:	2070 mm
Width:	678 mm
Dry weight:	165 kg
Wheelbase:	1440 mm
Fuel capacity:	23.9 litres

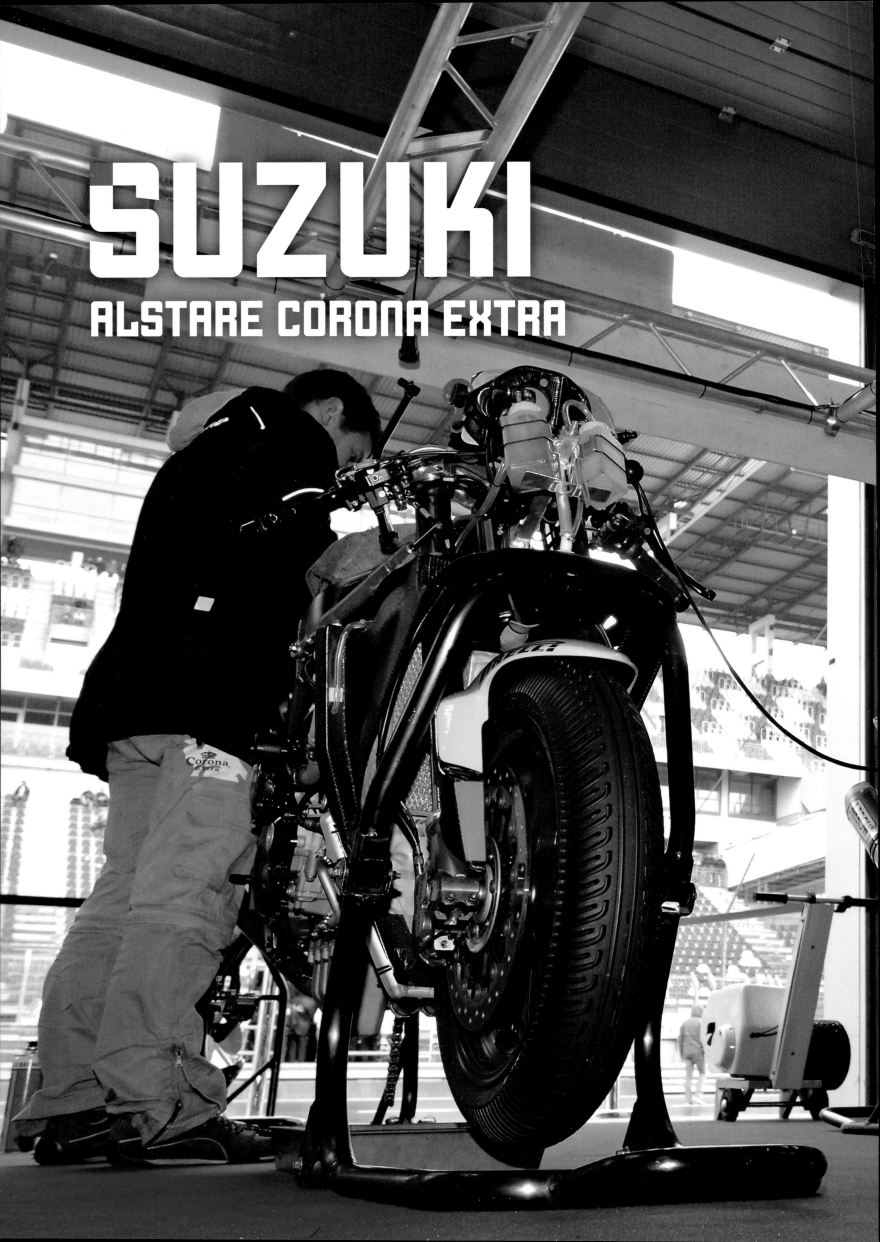

SUZUKI
ALSTARE CORONA EXTRA

Suzuki Alstare Corona Extra

Francis Batta is the man who more than anyone else personifies Super-bike. The Belgian manager has been involved in the category since the start, first as a promoter thanks to Diesel sponsorship, and then as a team owner who made his debut in Supersport in the mid-90s. In 1998 the team switched to Suzukis and entered Superbike the following year with Chili and Fujiwara. Continuing to believe in the category even when Suzuki (and many others...) had abandoned it, Batta together with his wife Patrizia and their squad had the satisfaction of winning the world title with Troy Corser in 2005. This season they took another gamble in bringing Max Biaggi to Superbike and the Italian repaid them with third place overall. The colourful and elegant livery of the Alstare team, which livens up not only the team garages but also the hospitality area and the entire paddock with the paddock show, will be replaced in 2008 with new colours, but Batta will continue to run one of the biggest, best and most competitive teams in Superbike.

Suzuki Alstare Corona Extra

ALSTARE SUZUKI CORONA EXTRA 2007	
Riders	Max Biaggi (# 3)
	Yukio Kagayama (# 71)
General Manager	Francis Batta
Team Coordinator	Yann Le Douche
R&D and Engine Director	Bruno Bailly
Press Officer	Kel Edge
Biaggi Crew	
Chief Mechanic	Giacomo Guidotti
Electronics Engineer	Massimo Neri
Engineer	Sebastien Delhaye
Mechanic	Christophe Marie-Sainte
Mechanic	Julien Armengaud
Mechanic	Jean-Francois Veitmann
Biaggi Crew	
Chief Mechanic	Dominique Dixneuf
Electronics Engineer	Stefano Ferro
Engineer	Yannick Pirotte
Mechanic	Cédric Véron
Mechanic	Vincent Bailly
Mechanic	Alessandro Veronesi
Storeman	Thierry Gerin

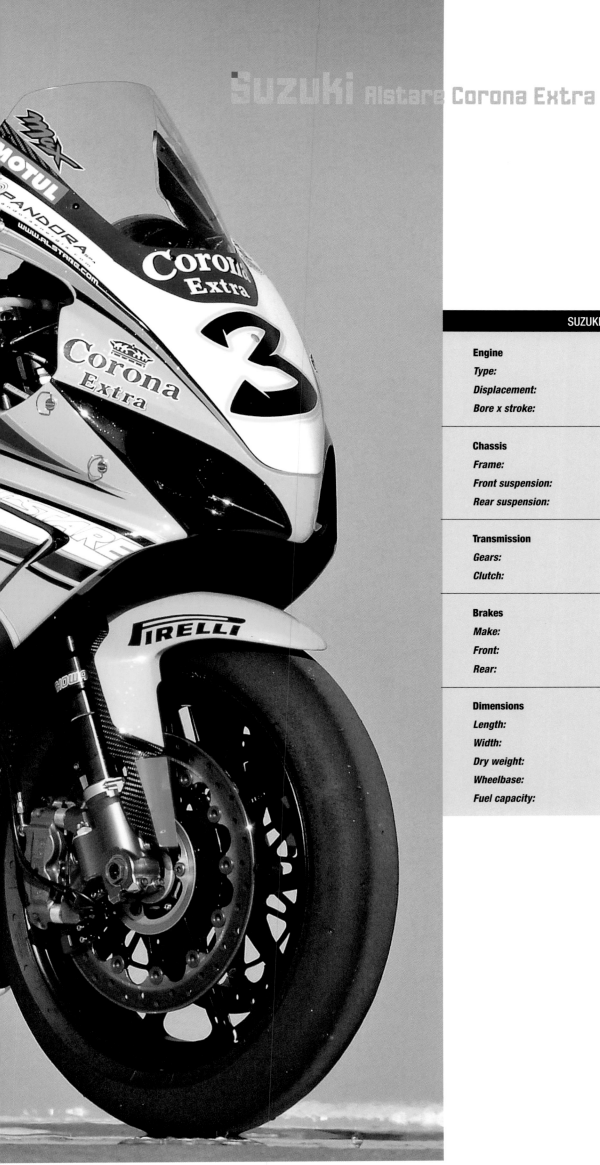

Suzuki Alstare Corona Extra

SUZUKI GSX-R1000 2007

Engine
Type:	four-cylinder, in-line
Displacement:	998,6 cc
Bore x stroke:	73,4 x 59 mm

Chassis
Frame:	aluminium twin-spar
Front suspension:	Showa upside-down forks
Rear suspension:	Showa single shock

Transmission
Gears:	six-speed
Clutch:	dry

Brakes
Make:	Brembo
Front:	320 mm twin disc
Rear:	220 mm single disc

Dimensions
Length:	n/a
Width:	n/a
Dry weight:	163 Kg
Wheelbase:	1455 mm
Fuel capacity:	23 litres

KAWASAKI
PSG-1 CORSE

Kawasaki PSG-1 Corse

Pier Guido Pagani is a keen racing enthusiast and in 2003 he decided to make his debut in Superbike by setting up a team for Pierfrancesco Chili with a Ducati 998. In 2005 together with a partner he made a further leap in quality by setting up a two-rider team, this time with Kawasaki bikes. Despite being present in Superbike almost since the beginning, Kawasaki has so far only won one world title (1993 with American Scott Russell) and the programme presented by the San Marino-based team immediately aroused the interest of the Japanese constructor who soon began to put all of its efforts behind the PSG-1 outfit. The squad run by Pagani entered two ZX10-RR machines in 2007 for Regis Laconi and Fonsi Nieto.

Kawasaki PSG-1 Corse

KAWASAKI PSG-1 TEAM 2007	
Riders	Fonsi Nieto (# 10
	Regis Laconi (# 55)
Principal Manager	Pierguido Pagani
Team Manager	Riccardo Varini
Sporting Director	Virginio Ferrari
Chief Mechanic	Massimo Tognacci
Press Officer	Sara Albani
Laconi Crew	
Head Mechanic	Pierluigi Aldrovandi
Electronics Technician	Massimo Tognacci
Mechanic	Alessandro Lazzarino
Mechanic	Daniele Penzo
Tyre Mechanic	Domenico Grieco
Nieto Crew	
Head Mechanic	Paolo Marchetti
Electronics Technician	Paolo Marchetti
Mechanic	Giancarlo Bosco
Mechanic	Lorenzo Gandino
Mechanic	Mattia Fontana
Tyre Mechanic	Michele Bubbolini
Hospitality	Andrea Valli
Logistics	Mahena Abbati

Kawasaki PSG-1 Corse

KAWASAKI ZX-10RR 2007	
Engine	
Type:	four-cylinder, in-line
Displacement:	998 cc
Bore x stroke:	76 x 55 mm
Valves:	four per cylinder
Power:	over 200 hp @ 14,000 rpm
Chassis	
Front suspension:	Ohlins inverted forks
Rear suspension:	Ohlins TTX single shock
Transmission	
Gears:	six-speed
Clutch:	wet, multiple disc
Brakes	
Make:	Brembo
Front:	2 x 320/310 mm
Rear:	218 mm
Dimensions	
Length:	n/a
Width:	n/a
Dry weight:	165 kg
Wheelbase:	n/a
Fuel capacity:	n/a

SUPERBIKE
Races

Troy Corser kicked off the 2007 season at the Losail circuit with pole position on his Yamaha R1. Right behind the Australian was the championship's latest big name arrival; Max Biaggi, after winning in MotoGP, surely had to be considered as one of the favourites for the title and the Suzuki Alstare Corona rider fully lived up to expectations with an amazing debut win in race 1 from Toseland. The others were nowhere, with Lanzi coming home third almost 14" behind. In race 2 James Toseland upheld the honour of the Superbike regulars, with a close win over Max, who almost came away with a double victory, while Corser finished third.

Phillip Island [Australia]

Superbike went down under to the magnificent Phillip Island circuit for the second round one week later and Ducati were immediately back on the pace with Troy Bayliss, who set the quickest time in Superpole. The Aussie and Toseland exchanged the top two places in the two races, with the others some way off the pace. Max Biaggi and Noriyuki Haga each picked up one third place and in a strange twist of fate, both also scored a fourth place finish. Thanks to these results, Toseland consolidated his lead in the championship, with Biaggi limiting the damage.

Donington [GB] / 01-04

Superbike's arrival in Europe for its twentieth anniversary event at Donington saw Bayliss and his Ducati grab a second successive Superpole, the Australian finishing ahead of Noriyuki Haga (Yamaha). Toseland (Honda) was unstoppable on his home circuit, the British rider winning race 1 by over a second from Corser. Things didn't go well for Bayliss however in the race as he crashed out and was taken to hospital with a damaged little finger, later amputated. Toseland was unable to take the double after he retired from race 2 with a mechanical problem while in the lead. Haga had to fight for the win with Biaggi (third in race 1), but he took the chequered flag ahead of the Italian and Yamaha team-mate Corser. Toseland was still leading the table by five points over Biaggi, who in turn had a good lead over Haga and Corser.

Just two weeks after his nasty Donington crash, Troy Bayliss was on pole at the Valencia circuit in Spain, just a fraction ahead of home favourite Ruben Xaus on another Ducati. Josh Brookes caused a surprise with third place on an Alto Evolution Honda. Spurred on by his home crowd, Xaus powered away to win race 1 by a clear margin from Haga and despite his injury, Bayliss finished third. The championship leaders were both behind but made amends in race 2 by taking the top two places. After a three-way battle, it was Toseland who took the win by a fraction from Biaggi and Haga, who was rapidly catching up at the top of the table, even though the British rider still had a 13-point lead over the Italian.

Assen (Netherland) / 29-04

An on-form Lorenzo Lanzi (Ducati) was just edged off the pole position by James Toseland, but was ahead of team-mate Bayliss. The early laps of race 1 were characterized by a battle between Toseland, Haga and Xaus, then the first two powered away and in the end it was the Ten Kate rider who got the better of his Japanese rival. For his part Ruben had the satisfaction of finishing ahead of the two factory Ducatis. Toseland rocketed into the lead of race 2 but was passed by Haga, who then had to retire mid-race with a technical problem. Bayliss took over at the front and the Australian had to defend his lead tooth and nail from Toseland right until the chequered flag. Toseland increased his championship lead, while Max Biaggi, thanks to Haga's retirement and a third place in race 2, remained second in the points table.

Monza [Italy] / 13-05

Proximity to team Headquarters must have given fresh impetus to Yamaha and it was Noriyuki Haga who clinched pole position, with Bayliss (Ducati), Biaggi (Suzuki) and Corser (Yamaha) also on the front row, while Toseland could only manage fifth place. It was Noriyuki's day however and the Samurai of Slide scored a fantastic double win at the high-speed Monza track, setting fastest lap in both races. Bayliss tried his hardest with the Ducati and scored a second and a third, while Biaggi (race 1) and Toseland (race 2) picked up the other two podium places. Haga was now ahead of Biaggi in the points table, with Bayliss catching up rapidly.

Silverstone [GB] / 27-05

Cold conditions, wind and rain characterized the Silverstone weekend for the second race this year in the UK. Bayliss, Haga and Toseland were at the top of qualifying, with Biaggi some places behind. Sunday's weather was dreadful and race 1 saw a clear win for Troy Bayliss (Ducati), who was now moving closer to the top of the table. The reigning world champion finished ahead of Haga who passed his team-mate Corser. Behind the two Yamahas came the second Honda Ten Kate rider, Roberto Rolfo, followed by Regis Laconi with a PSG-1 Kawasaki and Biaggi. Toseland crashed out without any serious consequences and rejoined the race to finish eighth. Race 2 was then called off because of the appalling weather conditions.

Misano (San Marino) / 17-06

Troy 'Mr Superpole' Corser added another notch to his record with pole at the revised Misano World Circuit, just one tenth of a second ahead of Bayliss. Ducati's Troy would be the man of the day however as he took a clear win in both races. Corser was second and Kagayama third, the Japanese rider stepping onto the podium for the first time this year, while Haga was taken out in a clash with Biaggi. In race 2 the podium was made up of Bayliss, Haga (Yamaha) and Biaggi (Suzuki). Toseland went home from Misano with a meagre fourth and sixth place, but was still in the lead, 21 points ahead of Bayliss who had moved ahead of Haga thanks to the double win.

Haga was the only rider to dip under the two minute mark in Brno qualifying but he was unable to make the most of his advantage in the race and despite setting fastest lap on both occasions, he had to settle for two fourths. From the mid-point of race 1 onwards James Toseland (Honda) took over at the front and went on to win, despite coming under pressure from Max Biaggi who settled for second. Yukio Kagayama was third with the second Suzuki-Alstare Corona machine. Max Biaggi dominated the second race, taking the chequered flag over a second ahead of Toseland. The podium was completed by the young Italian Michel Fabrizio with a Honda-DFX. In the championship Toseland still had a good lead, while Biaggi leapfrogged over Haga and Bayliss and was now second in the table.

The spectacular British track was the scene for a fantastic duel in Superpole between Bayliss and Toseland, who were separated by just three-hundredths of a second! Unfortunately the Ducati rider crashed in race 1, which put an end to his title defence, and handed the win to Toseland who was over one second ahead of Troy Corser at the flag; third place went to Max Biaggi who was trying not to lose contact with the championship leader. Haga had a great race but went off and finished seventh. Also in race 2 the 2004 world champion conceded nothing to his rivals and after holding off an attack from Haga went on to take his second win of the day, a result that virtually put a seal on the title battle.

Haga and Corser filled the other two podium positions on the podium. The Japanese rider was now second in the table ahead of Biaggi, who could only finish eighth after being penalized for a jump start.

A slippery track helped to give Fonsi Nieto (Kawasaki) a surprising pole position ahead of team-mate Regis Laconi. Troy Bayliss led until half-distance before his rear tyre went off and he had to leave the win to Haga. Biaggi (Suzuki) and Corser (Yamaha) finished second and third, eleven seconds behind, while Bayliss was fourth. It was exactly the same in the second race, with the Ducati rider again powering into the lead but then losing it to Haga at the mid-point when he made a small mistake. But this time the Australian returned to the front and stayed there until the chequered flag. Haga was runner-up for Yamaha, while Biaggi was some way behind in third, ahead of Toseland, whose points lead was slowly but surely being whittled away by his rivals.

Bayliss (Ducati) became the first rider to set pole position at the Vallelunga circuit on the outskirts of Rome, just a whisker ahead of Troy Corser (Yamaha), but it was local hero Max Biaggi who led for 21 of the 24 laps of the first race to take the track's first-ever World Superbike win. Bayliss finished runner-up, while Toseland was third and the other title contender Haga fourth. The incredible support of the Rome crowd was almost entirely for Biaggi but they also applauded a magnificent Troy Bayliss who led throughout race 2 to win from Biaggi. Haga was third, while Toseland could only finish eleventh.

Magny Cours [France] / 07-10

Three riders came to the French track with a chance of winning the title: Toseland, Biaggi and Haga. The championship leader set quickest time in qualifying, ahead of a surprising Neukirchner, while the others were further back. In race 1, Toseland could go no higher than seventh, while the win went easily to Nori Haga from team-mate Corser. Biaggi finished in sixth place and was now out of the race for the title, which boiled down to the battle between Haga and Toseland in race 2. The British rider, clearly tense before the start, had a 17 point lead over his Japanese rival, who knew he had to win to have a chance of taking the title. Toseland just managed to scrape though to the flag in sixth place, a result that allowed him to take his second WSBK title by two points! Biaggi and Fonsi Nieto, who finally had a competitive race for Kawasaki, took the other two podium slots.

SUPERSPORT
Champion

Kenan Sofuoglu

During the 2007 season Kenan So-
fuoglu turned into a true champion
and a rider to follow with interest in the future. Not only because he won the World
Supersport title, but for the way he won it,
with guts and determination as well as a
good dose of maturity.

The fact that he was the first Turkish rider
to win the world title helped to surround
him with a certain amount of media interest, probably to the detriment of all the other
technical and sporting aspects, but Kenan
managed to put things in the right perspec-
tive on the track with a string of victories.

Just a few facts and figures to start with:
Sofuoglu was born on August 25, 1983 in

Adapazari (Turkey) and is single. One hardly
notices his presence in the paddock as he is
a very reserved person. An orthodox Muslim,
Kenan defends his religion politely but firmly
and only talks about its positive aspects.

His racing career began at the start of the
new millennium, when he finished in second
place in the Supersport championship in
Turkey. In 2003 he again finished runner-up
in the Supersport championship, this time in
Germany, where he had moved to further his
career as a professional racer. The following
year he made his debut on the European
scene in the Superstock 1000 championship, where he finished third behind Lorenzo
Alfonsi and Gianluca Vizziello. 2005 saw him

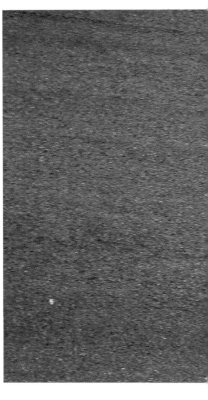

Kenan Sofuoglu

Kenan Sofuoglu

again take part in Superstock, and he finished runner-up behind his team-mate, Didier van Keymeulen from Belgium.

These results helped to open the doors to the best team in the Supersport category (despite scepticism in some areas), Honda Ten Kate, but Kenan immediately showed that he meant business with two wins in his rookie season at Assen and Lausitz), finishing third overall behind riders of the calibre of Charpentier and Curtain.

His confirmation in the Dutch team alongside the World Champion for the 2007 season was a foregone conclusion. This year Kenan won eight of the 13 rounds on

the calendar, clinching the Supersport 600 world title just four years after making his international debut. Now he can no longer be considered a curiosity or someone who 'arrived' thanks to his friendship with the Turkish Prime Minister...

For 2008 Sofuoglu is expected to move up to Superbike to face a new challenge and one that will certainly help to make motorcycling more popular in his country. At Brands Hatch and Magny-Cours there were about 20 or so of his fellow-countrymen to celebrate his world title, but the joy for the first Turkish champion was immense.

SUPERSPORT
Riders

The World Supersport Championship might have been totally dominated by Kenan Sofuoglu, but this doesn't means that there were no other leading contenders in the category that is intended to represent a feeder series for Superbike.

It was clear that this season there was a 'generation clash' between experienced riders such as Fujiwara, Foret, Charpentier and Nannelli and a series of younger 'guns' with less experience like Parkes, Jones, Roccoli and Harms.

After the opening salvo fired by 40-year-old Kevin Curtain (on a factory Yamaha) at the opening round in Qatar, it was then up to two riders who were over 30 years of age, Katsuaki Fujiwara (Honda–Althea) and Fab-

ien Foret (Kawasaki–Gil Motor), who won at Phillip Island, to try and contrast the Turkish champion. As well as these two veterans, two younger riders also made up the top positions in the standings: Australian Broc Parkes (on the other Yamaha factory bike) and Robin Harms from Denmark, both 25 years of age.

Parkes had two good races at Phillip Island and Valencia, but his attack on the title started at Misano and thanks to two wins at Brands Hatch and Lausitz, he finished a well-deserved runner-up in the final standings behind Sofuoglu.

Harms's season was the exact opposite, the Dane alternating a few good races with a lull in form that saw him drop from third to

Katsuaki Fujiwara

seventh place in the championship.

Fabien Foret made the most of his experience and managed to notch up the points, the Frenchman taking a third place overall ahead of Fujiwara from Japan, who stepped onto the podium three times with an Althea Honda.

Craig Jones (Revè Ekerold Honda Racing) turned into the real surprise of the season, especially towards the end when he scored three podiums. Massimo Roccoli, who held that honour in 2006, was unable to repeat his form of the previous year, when he won at Misano, but a sixth place overall confirmed him as the leading Italian this season.

Anthony West came, saw and conquered … and then left the series. Called in to replace an injured factory Yamaha rider, West scored a third place at Monza and then took two wins at Silverstone and Misano Adriatico. After this exploit, the Australian left the series to join the Kawasaki MotoGP team.

Also on the subject of Australian replacements, Andrew Pitt made the occasional appearance, the 2001 champion stepping onto the podium twice in one of the most competitive championships in motor cycle racing.

The Supersport grid was mainly made up of Japanese four-cylinder bike, but

Anthony West

Massimo Roccoli

there were also two twin-cylinder Ducatis, one of which was raced by Gianluca Nannelli. The Italian always raced at 100% and picked up a third place at Valencia and a fourth at Monza, but the 749R is clearly no longer able to compete with the Japanese bikes and the 33-year-old could only finish thirteenth overall.

SUPERSPORT
Races

Losail (Qatar)

Kevin Curtain's pole position for Yamaha gave the impression that the battle for the World Supersport Championship was going to have at least one other contender this year, but Kenan Sofuoglu took a different view and after Curtain's early attack, he took control on his Ten Kate Honda and went on to win. The Turkish rider's lead at the end was a comfortable one of over three seconds and he won from the factory Yamaha rider, who in turn finished in front of Katsuaki Fujiwara (Honda–Althea). The other Hannspree–Ten Kate rider, Frenchman Charpentier, crashed out with two laps remaining. Foret and Riba had a couple of good races for Kawasaki but finished some way off the podium.

Phillip Island (Australia)

Fabien Foret grabbed pole position for Kawasaki at the Phillip Island circuit, ahead of Curtain and Charpentier. In the race Australia's Broc Parkes (Yamaha) took the lead and stayed there for 18 of the 21 laps, leaving Charpentier in front for one lap. Then Foret made his move and took control, the Frenchman going on to win by seven-tenths of a second over Sofuoglu; the podium was completed by Parkes, who passed Charpentier, and Fujiwara, both on Hondas. The Hannspree-Ten Kate rider was now firmly in control in the championship standings, ahead of Foret on a Kawasaki.

Donington [GB]

Another Kawasaki rider, this time veteran Pere Riba, set quickest time in qualifying, while Simone Sanna was not far behind on a private Honda, the Italian qualifying ahead of Sofuoglu on the factory machine. Charpentier crashed, breaking his collarbone, and so did Parkes and Curtain. The race was run in two parts due to a crash, but the Turkish rider dominated from the lights to the flag to increase his championship lead. Denmark's Robbin Harms was seven-tenths behind in second, while Fujiwara completed an all-Honda podium, followed by two more CBR600RRs of Jones and Sanna in fourth and fifth place. Young Italian Davide Giugliano took the Kawasaki to sixth place.

Valencia (Spain)

Sofuoglu made his intentions for the Spanish round clear right from the start of first practice and the Turk took pole position by two-tenths of a second from veteran Fujiwara. The Ten Kate rider led almost throughout, leaving Curtain to lead for three laps, and he went on to win by over five seconds from Andrew Pitt who was replacing Charpentier on the second Honda of the Dutch team for this race. Gianluca Nannelli had a great race, taking the Ducati 749R to the final podium place. Fabien Foret finished fourth but was rapidly losing ground on championship leader Kenan Sofuoglu.

Assen (Netherland)

The Dutch round saw yet another pole position for Sofuoglu who was ahead of the returning Charpentier and Parkes, the best Yamaha rider. Any thoughts of a surprise result however soon fell by the wayside as Kenan attacked right from the start. The only rider able to stay in front of the Turk, albeit for four laps, was Pitt on the third Ten Kate Honda. Sofuoglu was totally dominant at Assen and was now over 50 points ahead of his rivals in the championship at the mid-point of the season. Behind Kenan, Pitt and Foret (Kawasaki) took the final two podium slots, the Frenchman now coming under pressure from Fujiwara for third place in the standings.

Monza (Italy)

Qualifying for the high-speed Monza race produced no real surprises except for the presence of Nannelli in the top positions and Kenan Sofuoglu was once again on pole position. Broc Parkes (Yamaha) led the early laps then a technical problem on his R6 halted his progress, and this left the championship leader with an undisturbed win (his fifth in six races) and a new circuit lap record. Four seconds behind was Frenchman Fabien Foret (Kawasaki), while Anthony West, star replacement on the second factory Yamaha, recovered well to finish runner-up. Nannelli scored a good fourth place finish on the Ducati 749R, but the rider from Tuscany came very close to the podium and was now fourth in the championship standings.

Silverstone [GB]

The outgoing world champion Sebastien Charpentier (Honda) showed that he was not going down without a fight at Silverstone as he grabbed pole position from Sofuoglu. The two Yamahas of Parkes and Roccoli were right behind the Honda CBR600RRs. The championship leader immediately crashed out of the race, leaving all the running to the Yamahas, first with Parkes (who also crashed) and then with Anthony West who powered to the win at the British circuit. For the second time this season, Harms stepped onto the podium after getting the better of Fuijwara. Foret finished fourth ahead of Vizziello to make up some ground on championship leader Sofuoglu, who now had a lead of 45 points.

Misano (San Marino)

Yamaha were now offering a much more serious challenge to the championship leader and their good form continued at Misano with the two R6 machines of Parkes and West up at the front in qualifying. Sofuoglu had a crash and lined up fourth behind Foret. West immediately powered into a commanding lead but the red flags came out after four laps. The second part of the race didn't change things however and it was the factory Yamaha stand-in rider who went on to win the race ahead of Sofuoglu, who lost out to Parkes on aggregate. Massimo Roccoli finished in fourth place on another Yamaha R6. In the points table Sofuoglu's lead was increasing over Foret, the Frenchman crashing out while third-placed Fujiwara was coming under pressure from Harms.

Brno (Czech Republic)

Sofuoglu was back on pole again at Brno with a record-breaking lap ahead of the two Australians Parkes and Brookes. Kenan was on flying form however and he won the 18-lap race with an advantage of over eleven seconds over the next man. Runner-up was the surprising Craig Jones (Honda), who clinched the place after Parkes and Harms were involved in a last-corner clash. Third place went to Fabien Foret who finished ahead of Massimo Roccoli on the leading Yamaha. The championship positions remained unchanged, but Sofuoglu's lead was increasing all the time.

Brands Hatch [Europe]

At Brands Hatch a Ten Kate Honda was again on pole but this time it was Charpentier up at the front, the Frenchman qualifying ahead of the other two CBR600RRs of Sofuoglu and Fuijwara. The championship leader got the best start but was immediately passed by Jones, who then crashed, and Parkes. The Australian won the race ahead of Sofuoglu, who settled for the championship points with the runner-up slot. The podium was completed by the young Italian Massimo Roccoli (Yamaha Team Italia) who was now level on points with Parkes. A second place was all that was required for Sofuoglu to take the title, the first ever won by a Turkish rider.

Lausitz (Germany)

The Hannspree–Ten Kate Hondas were at the front in qualifying, with Charpentier on pole. The race revolved around the battle between Broc Parkes (Yamaha) and Kenan Sofuoglu (Honda) who took turns in the lead. In the final stages the Australian was able to pull ahead and he won the race by almost two seconds from the Turk, who had brake problems. Frenchman Matthieu Lagrive (Honda) took the final podium slot with third place. With his win in Germany Parkes now moved into third in the championship ahead of Fujiwara.

Craig Jones, the young ex-Petronas SBK rider, surprisingly took pole position at the Rome circuit, ahead of Charpentier and Sofuoglu.

The first-ever race at Vallelunga however was won by Sofuoglu, who let Jones lead almost to the end before passing him for the win on the final lap.

A surprising third place went to Joan Lascorz (Honda) from Spain, who finished ahead of Parkes. The race was stopped before the end because of oil on the track.

Vallelunga (Italy)

Magny Cours (France)

Kenan Sofuoglu wanted to finish the season off in style and in qualifying he set pole position by a whisker from Parkes, his toughest opponent this year. The two riders took turns to lead the race, then the Turk decided that it was time to make a move and he broke away to win for the eighth time this year from the Australian. Jones was continuing his good end of season form and he finished on the podium after holding off the attacks from a determined Gianluca Vizziello who came home in fourth. With his second place at Magny-Cours, Parkes took the runner-up slot in the championship ahead of Foret, who retired in France. Thanks to his podium finish Jones moved up two places in the points table to finish fifth overall ahead of Roccoli and Harms.

SUPERSTOCK 1000

The final round of the FIM Superstock 1000 Cup at Magny-Cours had everything: a title that was won virtually at the last corner of the last lap, Ayrton Badovini showing what he was capable of after so much bad luck, Claudio Corti missing out on the title by a whisker, and joy for a well-deserved, last-minute triumph for Niccolò Canepa.

It was another outstanding season for the Superstock boys and once again the lion's share of the honours went to Italians. The only real interlopers were Xavier Simeon, who was not only born in Belgium but who is also now under the wing of the Belgian Alstare team, and 2004 champion Didier Van Keymeulen of the German MGM team.

Another name on everybody's lips was Australia's Mark Aitchison. Born in a small town on the Gold Coast, the youngster arrived in the squad run by Daniele Celani, the same group that had taken Alessandro Polita to the 2006 title, with a background of success in years of domestic racing. Without any knowledge of European circuits and no knowledge of Italian, he managed to integrate in the Rome-based team perfectly and work with clinical precision in his debut season. A couple of days to learn the tracks, the

warm-up on Sunday morning for final details and then the race, almost always spent in the group of front-runners. He only made a couple of errors, which however ended up by compromising his season: one was at Brands Hatch, when he misjudged the track entry time, and one was at Vallelunga when he crashed out of the title race. At twenty-four years of age, it will not be possible for him to repeat the Superstock experience,

but he is an emerging rider and is one step away from Superbike.

Niccolò Canepa on the other hand can be extremely proud of what he achieved in 2007. The rider from Liguria not only took a strategically important title for Ducati, with a debut win at Donington for the new 1098S and overall victory for a bike that will become the Italian manufacturer's next Superbike contender, but he also made a major contribution to the development of Borgo Panigale's new twin-cylinder machine. Canepa is a timid but determined young rider and managed not only to take the Ducati Xerox Junior Team to the top in Superstock, but also impressed factory Ducati management to such an extent that he was given the task of carrying out the first shakedown tests of the new 1200 machine and of notching up hundreds of kilometres of Desmosedici RR road-bike development testing at Mugello. Troy Bayliss also has a high opinion of him, which is always a good omen. Canepa is combining his racing with his studies however and after obtaining top marks in his school diploma, he has signed up for a university degree in Mechanical Engineering. Whatever happens from now on, Niccolò has a secure future ahead of him and is sure to go far…

For every winner, there is a loser and this time it was the turn of Claudio Corti. The rider from Como, who has been Canepa's adversary since minibikes, finished runner-up for the second time but this time round the disappointment must surely have been greater. Claudio is a tough rider, someone who is always game for a battle, as demonstrated by excellent results achieved in ice-hockey, a sport that is not exactly known for being for the faint-hearted. The Italian's low point of the season was Monza, where he scored no points and that made a big difference in the middle of the season. An injury in an Italian Championship race did the rest to deprive him of the necessary tranquillity to face up to the remaining rounds. At Magny-Cours he had to use all his race acumen and steely determination to bring home the result, and when Van Keymeulen crashed out it looked as if he was heading for victory until another Italian emerged to put paid to the Lorenzini rider's plans. His dreams were shattered when he was passed by Badovini in the last few kilometres.

Ayrton Badovini put paid to Corti's hopes of winning the title as he took the MV Agusta to its only victory of the season just a few corners away from the chequered flag. After Luca Scassa's performance the year before, the Italian manufacturer was hoping to fight for the title in 2007 but the end result was nowhere near expectations. Ayrton's win at the final race in some way made up for all the bad luck and errors committed during the season, but far too many crashes concealed his true potential.

Claudio Corti

Similar considerations can be made for Matteo Baiocco who led the table for much of the season. It is difficult to say exactly what happened in Baiocco's head but from Brands Hatch onwards he was no longer competitive after looking unbeatable in the early rounds.

Xavier Simeon was another talent to emerge on the Superstock scene. A protégé of Francesco Batta, the Belgian came to the Superstock 1000 category with the European title already in the bag and he didn't take long to acclimatise to the larger, more powerful machine. Eighteen years of age, a contract with one of the top teams in the championship in his hand, the rider from Brussels

can now calmly look forward to next season as being a crucial one for his future.

Ilario Dionisi, a Superstock regular, will no longer have this opportunity. For the rider from Rome, the 2007 season was his last chance as the age limit of 24 for the category means he has to move on. Dionisi has the physique to handle the heavier Superbike machines but he needs a budget and a team that can guarantee him a long-term future before stepping up.

Who knows what Michele Pirro and Brendan Roberts could have done if they had been in perfect condition. Both the Italian and the Australian, team-mates respec-

Matteo Baiocco

Xavier Simeon

tively for Corti and Canepa on a Yamaha and a Ducati, had serious injuries that ruined their seasons. Both have a good chance of returning to Superstock in 2008, when they will surely be amongst the favourites for the title.

Six years after it was created, the FIM Superstock 1000 Cup has seen the emergence of some talented new riders. The commitment of the manufacturers has also increased to the point that for them it has now become vitally important to be present in a series that has enormous repercussions on the market. However there are a number of considerations that need to be addressed. Getting onto the top of the podium has for some time now become increasingly difficult and teams and riders are called upon to be more and more professional. The problem is that after all these sacrifices, in most cases there are very few opportunities to step up to top-class Supersport or Superbike team structures. Ducati must be given a lot of credit for creating a Junior Team programme that has been copied by many other teams. Canepa might make the step up to greater things, but it is still not 100% sure. It is however important to guarantee a long-term future without asking the impossible from those without the necessary experience. If this is done, then the Superstock 1000 Cup will have carried out its job of creating the champions of the future.

Ilario Dionisi

Michele Pirro

Didier Vankeymeulen

Ayrton Badovini

Brendan Roberts

SUPERSTOCK
600

It goes without saying that the level of quality in the European Superstock 600 Championship is growing year after year.

For the past three seasons, the category reserved for young riders from 14 to 20 years of age has been an integral part of the Superbike event programme and it has perfectly carried out the job it was designed to do: produce the champions of the future.

Looking back on the championship results of the last few years it is easy to identify the names of those riders who after leaving Superstock 600, have gone on to make a name for themselves in the higher categories.

For example, this year Claudio Corti, the 2005 championship winner, was still in with a chance of fighting for the FIM Superstock 1000 Cup title right down to the final round. In the end this particular title went to another Italian rider who stood out in last year's European championship, Niccolò Canepa. Yoann Tiberio, Corti's chief rival in 2005, was also one of the protagonists of last season's World Supersport championship, the young

Frenchman even scoring a win, while this year he took part in the last few rounds of the Superbike championship, even making it into Superpole.

The same can be said for Xavier Simeon: champion in 2006, the Belgian remained in the orbit of the team with the biggest budget in Superbike, Francis Batta's Alstare Corona Extra outfit, battling for victory with Canepa and Corti in the Superstock 1000 Cup. The category appears to be doing its job to perfection.

The 2007 championship was even more exciting than the previous year's one. First, let's have a look at a few numbers: 42 riders were down on the final entry-list for the European championship, with 21 'wild-cards' who took turns in competing in the 11 rounds of the season. This was a fantastic turn-out for a category widely considered to be a true training-ground for the various production bike-based racing series.

28 teams were officially entered, with 17 others ready to step in with 'wild-card' entries; not a bad result indeed for a class that

Maxime Berger

saw 10 teams take part in the 2007 series with two riders.

The racing also stepped up a gear as well, with lap times diminishing by an average of over two-and-a-half seconds in almost all the European races throughout 2006.

The season kicked off in Donington, where Italian colours were in evidence and where Michele Magnoni, a 19-year-old making his debut in the category with a Bevilacqua Corse Yamaha R6, got the better of Antonelli (Italia Megabike Honda) and Colucci (Ducati Xerox Junior Team) in the opening round.

From Valencia onwards however, the pairing of Maxime Berger and Team Trasimeno began to exert its supremacy on the championship battle. Returning to Superstock 600 after racing a Kawasaki Supersport in 2006, the 18-year-old rider from Dijon won the Spanish race from Ten Napel and Rea. He then finished third at Assen behind Antonelli and Barrier and won at Misano from Magnoni and 'wild-card', Bussolotti.

At Monza Magnoni took the win, and it was clear that he, together with Antonelli and Colucci, was Berger's chief rival for the title. After the Frenchman's victory at Misano and Domenico Colucci's win at Brno, the spectacular and difficult Brands Hatch circuit proved to be the decider in the battle for the title.

With the Silverstone round re-scheduled for Brands after being rained off in May, Maxime Berger picked up a double win in the UK, ahead of Colucci and Magnoni in race 1 and Antonelli and Black in the second race of the week-end. Unfortunately Colucci's season ended there as he crashed out and broke his leg. The double win allowed Berger to increase his points lead and head towards the European title.

In a confusing race held under a downpour at the Eurospeedway in Germany, Lonbois took a surprise win for Suzuki while Berger clinched the title at Vallelunga with third place behind winner Ten Napel and Antonelli.

Andrea Antonelli

Berger then celebrated his season in the best possible way with a win over Antonelli and Black in front of 50,000 fans at his home circuit of Magny-Cours. In the final round Andrea Antonelli overtook Magnoni in the fight for the runner-up slot in the championship.

With eight wins to its name in 2007, Yamaha again proved to be the bike to beat in the European Superstock 600 Championship, while one win apiece went to its rivals, Ducati, Honda and Suzuki. For its part Team Trasimeno scored its second win in the category following Corti's triumph in 2005.

Superstock again did its job in 2007, and will undoubtedly prove to be an important 'feeder' category for all the other classes. Berger, Antonelli, Magnoni, Colucci, Black, Ten Napel and Barrier are just some of the names who could go on to bigger things in Supersport and Superstock 1000 in 2008.

Greg Black

Sylvain Barrier

Vincent Lonbois

Daniele Beretta

Marco Bussolotti

Twenty years old!
It seems like just yesterday that Superbike
made its debut on the world scene.
Things were difficult at first, but the category
soon established itself as an important addition
to international motorbike racing.
A multitude of riders and key figures have
held stage in the world championship for
production-based machinery, some of which
have left an important mark,
others sinking without trace.
In the next few pages we have tried to sum
up in images the most significant moments of
the past seasons of Superbike racing, so that
our memories can help us to better appreciate
the past and above all the future.

SUPERBIKE History

THE EARLY YEARS

Races for bikes based on production machines have their origins in the mists of time but they only started to become well-known in the 1970s, when in some countries (in particular USA and Australia) Superbike races were organized. These were strictly for large-cylinder (up to 1100 cc) four-stroke bikes.

The races in the United States, for example, were characterised by the first legendary battles between Kawasaki, BMW, Ducati and a few Moto Guzzis with riders of the calibre of Yvon Du Hamel, Steve McLaughlin, Cook Neilson, Ron Pierce, Mike Baldwin (who also raced a Moto Guzzi) and Wes Cooley. They had massive success, but the arrival of Grand Prix bikes in the United States, and their subsequent replacement by 700 cc and 750 cc two-stroke, three or four-cylinder machines, cast a shadow over this category for a short while.

At the end of the 1970s the AMA (American Motorcyclist Association) decided to once again put their backing behind four-stroke production-based machines by creating Superbike. For a short while the European bikes managed to hold off the Japanese machines but then technology from the Far East got the upper hand. This was the period of the Yoshimura-tuned Suzuki 1000 bikes of Pierce, Cooley (multiple AMA champion) and Emde, who were up against the Kawasakis of Pridmore and McLaughlin and the BMWs of Long and Klinzmann.

The real boom came in the 1980s when several new faces entered the Superbike championship: Eddie Lawson on a Kawasaki, and Freddie Spencer on a Honda. Lawson beat his rival in 1981 while the following year there was no repeat match because Spencer preferred to move on to GP racing, after winning the opening round of the season held at Daytona.

Now the battles were restricted to the Japanese machines (Honda, Kawasaki

and Suzuki), while the success of Superbike was finally beginning to make its way over in Europe, first with the legendary Transatlantic Trophy races and then thanks to the unforgettable Francesco "Checco" Costa, who wanted Superbikes as a spectacular support race to his Imola 200 Miles in 1981 and 1982. For the record, in 1981 Wes Cooley with a Suzuki-Yoshimura got the better of Roberto Pietri on a Honda, while the following year Pietri won from Italian Maurizio Massimiani on an endurance Honda.

Until 1987 the list of AMA champions was made up of names that were also famous in Europe: Wayne Rainey (1983-1987) and Fred Merkel (1984-1985-1986) and the same could be said for the other top riders like Kevin Schwantz, John Kocinski and Bubba Shobert. While in America the riders 'launched' by Superbike opted to enter Grand Prix racing, the Europeans were discovering… America!

In 1987 a Superbike Trophy was organised in Italy and it was won by Fabrizio Pirovano (in the Sport category) and by Mauro Ricci (Production), but the real stars of the championship were Marco Lucchinelli (Ducati 851) and Fred Merkel (who raced with an Italian licence on a Team Servisco Honda VFR). The Trophy, thanks to the expert organisation of Flammini Racing, had an excellent impact on the general public and was a guiding factor in the launch of the world championship in 1988.

WORLD SUPERBIKE CHAMPIONS			
1988	FRED MERKEL	USA	HONDA
1989	FRED MERKEL	USA	HONDA
1990	RAYMOND ROCHE	F	DUCATI
1991	DOUG POLEN	USA	DUCATI
1992	DOUG POLEN	USA	DUCATI
1993	SCOTT RUSSELL	USA	KAWASAKI
1994	CARL FOGARTY	GBR	DUCATI
1995	CARL FOGARTY	GBR	DUCATI
1996	TROY CORSER	AUS	DUCATI
1997	JOHN KOCINSKI	USA	HONDA
1998	CARL FOGARTY	GBR	DUCATI
1999	CARL FOGARTY	GBR	DUCATI
2000	COLIN EDWARDS	USA	HONDA
2001	TROY BAYLISS	AUS	DUCATI
2002	COLIN EDWARDS	USA	HONDA
2003	NEIL HODGSON	GBR	DUCATI
2004	JAMES TOSELAND	GBR	DUCATI
2005	TROY CORSER	AUS	SUZUKI
2006	TROY BAYLISS	AUS	DUCATI
2007	JAMES TOSELAND	GBR	HONDA

1988

A world championship finally got underway one year later than announced by the FIM due to teething problems. Nine rounds were on the calendar, including six in Europe and the other three in Japan, Australia and New Zealand. Notable for its absence was Italy, which in these early stages did not believe much in Superbike despite the existence of a domestic trophy. The first world champion was the American Fred Merkel who proved to be the true 'king' of the category on a Honda VFR of the Italian Rumi team, winning two races. His most serious rival was surprisingly the

former motocross racer Fabrizio Pirovano (Yamaha FZR 750) who finished runner-up just five and a half points behind, winning amongst others the race at the prestigious Le Mans circuit. The two Bimota YB4s of Davide Tardozzi (who was the first winner of a Superbike race in the history of the world championship) and Stephane Mertens and the Ducati 851 of Marco Lucchinelli (first winner of a round, because Donington was run on aggregate results) had various problems, leaving the American to take the world title. The outcome was disappointing for the Italians, who stepped onto the top of the podium five times (Tardozzi), twice (Lucchinelli) and once Pirovano. It is worth mentioning that a certain Mick Doohan on a Yamaha

Marco Lucchinelli

won one race at Sugo and two at Oran Park (Australia).

1° F. MERKEL	USA	HONDA	99
2° F. PIROVANO	ITA	YAMAHA	93,5
3° D. TARDOZZI	ITA	BIMOTA	91,5
4° S. MERTENS	BEL	BIMOTA	90,5
5° M. LUCCHINELLI	ITA	DUCATI	64
6° A. VIEIRA	FRA	HONDA	42
7° R. PHILLIS	AUS	KAWASAKI	42
8° G. GOODFELLOW	CAN	SUZUKI	39,5
9° M. CAMPBELL	AUS	HONDA	33,5
10° T. RYMER	GBR	HONDA	32,5

Davide Tardozzi

Fred Merkel

1989

The calendar was expanded to eleven races with the addition of two overseas rounds in the USA and Canada. Despite the promoter going bankrupt, Superbike managed to carry on and demonstrate its true worth. The same could be said for Fred Merkel (Honda) who won his second successive world title in the end by defeating Stephane Mertens on a similar machine. Ducati were becoming increasingly competitive in the hands of the tough

French expert Raymond Roche, whose team-mate was Baldassarre Monti. It was also a positive season for Fabrizio Pirovano who was the best Yamaha rider and the Italian finished ahead of Andersson from Sweden and Rymer from Britain. Suzuki scored its first world championship win in the hands of Doug Polen, but the revelation of the season was Giancarlo Falappa on a competitive Bimota machine, who won three races in England, Canada and France.

Fred Merkel

1° F. MERKEL	USA	**HONDA**	272
2° S. MERTENS	BEL	**HONDA**	265
3° R. ROCHE	FRA	**DUCATI**	222
4° F. PIROVANO	ITA	**YAMAHA**	208
5° A. ANDERSSON	SWE	**YAMAHA**	159
6° G. C. FALAPPA	ITA	**BIMOTA**	139
7° T. RYMER	GBR	**HONDA**	134
8° B. MONTI	ITA	**DUCATI**	99
9° J. SUHONEN	FIN	**YAMAHA**	90
10° M. DOWSON	AUS	**YAMAHA**	79
10° R. PHILLIS	AUS	**KAWASAKI**	79

Raymond Roche

Fred Merkel

Giancarlo Falappa

Honda 1989

1990

World Superbike made a major step forward in 1990 when the Flammini Group took over the organisation and developed a series of programmes that would lead to the definitive emergence of the championship. A helping-hand in this was provided by the victory of Raymond Roche on a Ducati 851, one of the few bikes made in Europe that proved to be capable of challenging Japanese supremacy. The Frenchman encountered a number of tough rivals throughout the season, including the two Honda riders, Fred Merkel and Stephane Mertens, as well as Fabrizio Pirovano (Yamaha). The Italian finished the season strongly and picked up the runner-up slot ahead of Mertens and Australia's Rob Phillis on a Kawasaki. Ducati also scored a historic victory at the Sugo circuit in Japan on the Japanese manufacturers' home ground.

Raymond Roche

1° R. ROCHE	FRA	**DUCATI**	391
2° F. PIROVANO	ITA	**YAMAHA**	337
3° S. MERTENS	BEL	**HONDA**	321
4° R. PHILLIS	AUS	**KAWASAKI**	252
5° R. McELNEA	GBR	**YAMAHA**	236
6° F. MERKEL	USA	**HONDA**	197
7° T. RYMER	GBR	**YAMAHA**	169
8° B. MONTI	ITA	**HONDA**	149
9° A. ANDERSSON	SWE	**YAMAHA**	159
10° J. SUHONEN	FIN	**YAMAHA**	90

Stephane Mertens

Fabrizio Pirovano

1991

Texan Doug Polen burst onto the World Superbike Championship scene with wins in the opening rounds in England and Spain; his Donington victory would be the first of six double wins that year. At the end of the season Polen had won 17 races out of 26 on the calendar! The Fast by Ferracci riders' title victory was a foregone conclusion, and it gave Ducati a second Superbike crown in a row. Outgoing champion Raymond Roche (Ducati) underestimated his American rival at the start of the season and had an uphill struggle for the rest of the year. Roche only came on strong at the end of the season to finish runner-up behind Polen. The other riders who stood out in 1991

were Rob Phillis with a rapidly-improving Kawasaki and Stephane Mertens in his debut year with Ducati after several seasons with Honda. The season was also noteworthy for the arrival of Scott Russell (Kawasaki), who scored two second places in the United States round, the first races for a young New Zealander Aaron Slight, who scored a third and fourth place in Japan, and the riders' refusal to race at Mosport because the track was too dangerous. Carl Fogarty also took part in several races on a Honda RC30, and the British rider finished seventh overall. A European championship was run together with the world championship and was won by Davide Tardozzi on a Ducati.

Doug Polen

1° D. POLEN	USA	DUCATI	432
2° R. ROCHE	FRA	DUCATI	282
3° R. PHILLIS	AUS	KAWASAKI	267
4° S. MERTENS	BEL	DUCATI	217
5° F. PIROVANO	ITA	YAMAHA	195
6° T. RYMER	GBR	YAMAHA	162
7° C. FOGARTY	GBR	HONDA	146
8° F. MERKEL	USA	HONDA	124
9° G.C. FALAPPA	ITA	DUCATI	113
10° D. TARDOZZI	ITA	DUCATI	108

Rob Phillis

Doug Polen

1992

Anyone who thought Doug Polen's victory was a flash in the pan had to think again as the American won nine of the 26 races in the 1992 championship to take his second successive world title. This time round it wasn't easy however as Roche tried to take back the title before retiring, but in the end the Frenchman again had to settle for the runner-up slot. The Ducatis were now starting to dominate in World Superbike but they were gradually being challenged by Kawasaki. After a first victory for Aaron Slight at Albacete, the Japanese manufacturer also took two more victories at Spa and Jarama (with Phillis). Italians Giancarlo Falappa (Ducati) and Fabrizio Pirovano (Yamaha) also had a good year, but it was Slight who stood out in his first full year of World Superbike racing. These three finished in that order behind Polen, Roche and 'veteran' Rob Phillis.

Doug Polen

1° D. POLEN	USA	**DUCATI**	371
2° R. ROCHE	FRA	**DUCATI**	336
3° R. PHILLIS	AUS	**KAWASAKI**	289
4° G.C. FALAPPA	ITA	**DUCATI**	279
5° F. PIROVANO	ITA	**YAMAHA**	278
6° A. SLIGHT	NZE	**KAWASAKI**	249
7° S. MERTENS	BEL	**DUCATI**	182
8° D. AMATRIAN	ESP	**DUCATI**	156
9° C. FOGARTY	GBR	**DUCATI**	134
10° P.L. BONTEMPI	ITA	**KAWASAKI**	125

Raymond Roche

Rob Phillis

1993

After taking part in a couple of US rounds when World Superbike came to America, in 1993 Scott Russell decided to do the whole season with the Rob Muzzy-run team that had taken him to victory in the 1992 AMA championship. His main rivals were first Giancarlo Falappa and then Carl Fogarty with the Ducatis, but in the end the Kawasaki rider managed to take the title ahead of 'Foggy' and Kawasaki team-mate Aaron Slight. Fourth place went to Fabrizio Pirovano, who left Yamaha at the end of the season to switch to Ducati. One of the sur-

prises of 1993 was Austrian Andreas Meklau who won his home race in the wet against all odds, but also managed to put together some other good results. The revelation of the season however was the former motocross racer from Padua, Mauro Lucchiari, who scored some good results on a 'private' (but later factory-assisted) Ducati 888, finishing tenth overall. The Riders' title went to Kawasaki, while Ducati had to settle for the Manufacturers' crown with the 888, a bike that would be pensioned off at the end of the season to make way for the 916, which had been launched at the Milan Show.

Scott Russell

1° S. RUSSELL	USA	**KAWASAKI**	378,5
2° C. FOGARTY	GBR	**DUCATI**	349,5
3° A. SLIGHT	NZE	**KAWASAKI**	316
4° F. PIROVANO	ITA	**YAMAHA**	290
5° G.C. FALAPPA	ITA	**DUCATI**	255
6° P.L. BONTEMPI	ITA	**KAWASAKI**	184,5
7° S. MERTENS	BEL	**DUCATI**	172
8° T. RYMER	GBR	**YAMAHA**	116
9° C. LINDHOLM	SWE	**YAMAHA**	102
10° M. LUCCHIARI	ITA	**DUCATI**	94,5

Carl Fogarty

KAWASAKI 1993

1994

1994 was one of the greatest ever Superbike seasons. Three riders fought for the title right down to the final round: Carl Fogarty with the new Ducati 916, Scott Russell with the Kawasaki ZXR750 that had won the championship the previous year and Aaron Slight with a bike making its WSBK debut, the Honda RC45. Until the San Marino Round at Misano, there were four contenders for the title, but a nasty crash at Albacete during private testing brought an end to the hopes and the career of Giancarlo Falappa, who still today bears the consequences of that unfortunate accident. Another major upset was the disqualification of Slight (and Meklau) after the opening round at Donington for illegal fuel. The FIM ruling on the matter took ages to be issues and

this conditioned the entire championship. Scott Russell powered away in the first four races, but Fogarty kept his cool and began his charge with two wins at the Albacete circuit in Spain. This was immediately followed by another one at Zeltweg and at this point the championship battle was wide open. The occasional help from team-mates or fellow Ducati riders Andy Meklau, Marco Lucchiari, Jamie Whitham, Troy Corser (who, together with Kawasaki's Anthony Gobert was the revelation of the season) allowed "Foggy" to move into the lead of the standings. Russell responded with a double win at Sugo, but an absurd FIM ruling on the illegal fuel situation allowed Slight to move back to the top of the table. Shortly afterwards the New Zealander then had his points docked. The championship's return to Europe allowed Fogarty to take control of the situation once again, but neither Russell nor Slight was giv-

Carl Fogarty

ing up easily. A textbook race at the Phillip Island circuit gave Carl Fogarty his first World Superbike title.

1° C. FOGARTY	GBR	DUCATI	305
2° S. RUSSELL	USA	KAWASAKI	280
3° A. SLIGHT	NZE	HONDA	277
4° D. POLEN	USA	HONDA	158
5° S. CRAFAR	NZE	HONDA	153
6° A. MEKLAU	AUT	DUCATI	148
7° J. WHITHAM	GBR	DUCATI	126
8° P.L. BONTEMPI	ITA	KAWASAKI	116
9° F. PIROVANO	ITA	DUCATI	111
10° T. RYMER	GBR	KAWASAKI	106

Aaron Slight

1995

Pole position for the Ducati 916 at the ultra-fast Hockenheim track was a clear sign that nothing had changed from the previous year. With two more 916s right behind, Ducati were favourites for victory. The pole went to Troy Corser, the young Australian who had just won the AMA title, and who had been signed by the Promotor team; Troy was a fraction ahead of another new Superbike star, Pierfrancesco Chili (Gattolone-Ducati) and reigning world champion Fogarty (Ducati-Ferrari). The British rider wasted no time in stamping his authority and dominated both races with a perfectly-functioning Ducati 916 machine.

The German Round was the first of a se-

ries of four double wins that Fogarty scored that year as he powered to his second successive World Superbike title.

Ducati's wins that year, when the Italian factory notched up the 100 mark, also came from Mauro Lucchiari (Ducati-Ferrari) who won both rounds at Misano; Pierfrancesco Chili at Monza with the first win for the Gattolone team in Superbike, and also from Troy Corser, who was clearly destined to be a serious challenger for the title in 1996.

After losing Russell, who moved to 500 GP a third of the way through the season, Kawasaki's fortunes were in the hands of Anthony Gobert, who won at Laguna Seca and Phillip Island.

Thanks to Aaron Slight, the Honda RC45 took its first win at Albacete but apart from another win at Sentul the four-cylinder Jap-

Carl Fogarty

anese bike was unable to offer much of a challenge that season.

Yamaha lost their star Yasutomo Nagai two laps from the end of the second race at

1° C. FOGARTY	GBR	**DUCATI**	478
2° T. CORSER	AUS	**DUCATI**	339
3° A. SLIGHT	NZE	**HONDA**	323
4° A. GOBERT	AUS	**KAWASAKI**	222
5° Y. NAGAI	JPN	**YAMAHA**	188
6° S. CRAFAR	NZE	**HONDA**	187
7° F. PIROVANO	ITA	**DUCATI**	178
8° P.F. CHILI	ITA	**DUCATI**	160
9° M. LUCCHIARI	ITA	**DUCATI**	156
10° J. REYNOLDS	GBR	**KAWASAKI**	155

Pierfrancesco Chili

Aaron Slight

Assen when he crashed and his bike incredibly came down on top of him at a circuit considered to be one of the safest in the world.

The best results for the Japanese team, which abandoned the last rounds of the season out of mourning, were a second place for Edwards at Brands Hatch and the same result for Nagai at Sugo.

Corser, Lucchiari, Fogarty

DUCATI 1995

1996

John Kocinski (Ducati) burst on-to the World Superbike scene with a vengeance with a double win in the opening round held at Misano's Santamonica circuit. His rivals didn't take much time to get over the shock of the former 250 world champion's arrival and Troy Corser, who was also on a factory Ducati but in a different team, responded with a double win at Donington.

The championship then became more interesting with a double victory for Honda at Hockenheim, where Slight and Fogarty took a win apiece with the RC45. Chili also won at Monza and Brands Hatch and Gobert took the Laguna Seca race win.

The championship arrived at the final stages with four riders in a position to win the world title: Corser and Kocinski on Ducatis and Slight and Fogarty on Hondas. Things turned sour between the American and his Ducati team however and this certainly did not help to give Kocinski the necessary harmony for his attack on the title.

At Albacete, Corser won both races to become the favourite as they headed to the final round at Phillip Island. The Australian scored a third place in the first race, which was all that was required for him to take the 1996 title. His rivals were unable to offer much of a challenge and Gobert, unbeatable on his home circuit, took both the race wins.

1° T. CORSER	AUS	DUCATI	369
2° A. SLIGHT	NZE	HONDA	347
3° J. KOCINSKI	USA	DUCATI	337
4° C. FOGARTY	GBR	HONDA	331
5° C. EDWARDS	USA	YAMAHA	248
6° P.F. CHILI	ITA	DUCATI	223
7° S. CRAFAR	NZE	KAWASAKI	180
8° A. GOBERT	AUS	KAWASAKI	167
9° W. YOSHIKAWA	JON	YAMAHA	163
10° N. HODGSON	GBR	DUCATI	122

Carl Fogarty

John Kocinski

Troy Corser

1997

After Troy Corser had made the move to 500 GP (where he was unable to have much success), the 1997 Superbike season got underway with Kocinski and Fogarty switching bikes and Russell (Yamaha) back on a four-stroke machine again.

Kocinski started off well in Australia and with a win in the second race at Misano moved into the lead of the championship. Slight and Chili both scored wins in the opening rounds and the battle for the title was wide-open. Kocinski failed to go well at Donington and Fogarty took advantage to take over at the top, followed by Slight. These three were now starting to pull ahead and they increased their lead at Hockenheim, with Crafar the only one offering much

resistance. Chili (Ducati) scored his usual win at Monza, but the other victory went to Kocinski who passed Slight in the points table and moved closer to Fogarty.

Chili and Russell were competitive on occasions but Kocinski and Fogarty were virtually unstoppable as they shared the wins at Laguna Seca. Fogarty won at Brands but a second and a third allowed Kocinski to overtake him at the top. Fogarty scored a win and a DNF in Austria while Kocinski was slowly notching up the points. Yanagawa (Kawasaki) scored his first win at Zeltweg to move ahead of his team-mate Crafar, who was slipping away after a good first half of the season. At Assen Fogarty and Kocinski again shared the wins and they went to Albacete separated by two points. Slight was third, 60 points behind.

Kocinski's double win in Spain was a

John Kocinski

severe blow to the hopes of Fogarty and Ducati. Chili moved into fourth place ahead of Russell, while Crafar was again back on form and overtook Yanagawa.

Neither of the two title favourites went

1° J. KOCINSKI	USA	HONDA	416
2° C. FOGARTY	GBR	DUCATI	358
3° A. SLIGHT	NZE	HONDA	243
4° A. YANAGAWA	JPN	KAWASAKI	247
5° S. CRAFAR	NZE	KAWASAKI	234
6° S. RUSSELL	USA	YAMAHA	226
7° P.F. CHILI	ITA	DUCATI	209
8° J. WHITHAM	GBR	SUZUKI	140
9° N. HODGSON	GBR	DUCATI	137
10° P.L. BONTEMPI	ITA	KAWASAKI	118

Carl Fogarty

well in Japan, but Kocinski took the title at Sugo with an eighth place and a third. Fogarty raced for pride in the remaining two rounds and won the final race of the season in Indonesia, with Kocinski taking the other win. Slight finished third, while a win at Sugo propelled Yanagawa into fourth place in his first world championship year, ahead of Crafar, Russell and Chili in seventh.

Slight, Kocinski

1998

The 23-year-old Japanese rider Noriyuki Haga burst onto the world scene and was immediately competitive with a factory Yamaha against Carl Fogarty, who was aiming for his third world title. Unfortunately Haga crashed at Monza and this left the way clear for Colin Edwards, who had switched to Honda after a couple of years with Yamaha.

Corser (Ducati) also looked competitive but Fogarty was on top form and after a mid-season crisis he put together a string of results that allowed him to win the title for the third time.

Aaron Slight came on strong during the mid-season races but had to settle for the runner-up slot, just 4.5 points behind Fogarty. Chili had a good season and scored wins at Albacete, Nurburgring and Assen and a double victory at Kyalami.

Carl Fogarty

1° C. FOGARTY	GBR	DUCATI	351,5
2° A. SLIGHT	NZE	HONDA	347
3° T. CORSER	AUS	DUCATI	328,5
4° P.F. CHILI	ITA	DUCATI	293,5
5° C. EDWARDS	USA	HONDA	279,5
6° N. HAGA	JPN	YAMAHA	258
7° A. YANAGAWA	JPN	KAWASAKI	210
8° J. WHITHAM	GBR	SUZUKI	173
9° P. GODDARD	AUS	SUZUKI	155
10° S. RUSSELL	USA	YAMAHA	130,5

Fogarty, Slight, Corser

Noriyuki Haga

1999

Carl Fogarty won his fourth World Superbike title in 1999 on a Ducati 996 and dominated so convincingly that he was more than 130 points ahead of second-placed Colin Edwards (Honda) and Troy Corser (Ducati) in the standings. Edwards and Corser were quite simply unable to do anything about the British rider, who won 11 races compared with 5 for the American and 3 for the Australian.

Aaron Slight (Honda) and Akira Yanagawa (Kawasaki) both scored good results to finish fourth and fifth overall, with the Japanese rider scoring the Green Team's only win. Chili, who had moved to Suzuki, scored two wins at Zeltweg and Hockenheim.

Carl Fogarty

1°	C. FOGARTY	GBR	DUCATI	489
2°	C. EDWARDS	USA	HONDA	361
3°	T. CORSER	AUS	DUCATI	361
4°	A. SLIGHT	NZE	HONDA	323
5°	A. YANAGAWA	JPN	KAWASAKI	308
6°	P.F. CHILI	ITA	SUZUKI	251
7°	N. HAGA	JPN	YAMAHA	196
8°	G. LAVILLA	ESP	KAWASAKI	156
9°	K. FUJIWARA	JPN	SUZUKI	119
10°	V. GUARESCHI	ITA	YAMAHA	99

Colin Edwards

Fogarty e Slight

2000

A nasty crash brought an end to the series of title wins for "Foggy", who was unable to recover fully from his injury and had to retire from racing. It was a severe blow for Superbike and for Ducati.

The first title of the second millennium deservedly went to Colin Edwards (on the new Honda VTR), who came to SBK in 1995 with Yamaha and who switched to Honda three years later. The American won eight races. One of the favourites was Haga, but a problem with doping (never entirely cleared up) put an end to his hopes. The season was also notable for the emergence of Australian Troy Bayliss, who had been called in by Ducati from the AMA series and who surprisingly finished sixth overall.

Another Australian, Troy Corser, had a positive year in his first season with the Aprilia RSV1000, winning five races, while Anthony Gobert scored a surprising win on a Bimota at Phillip Island; unfortunately the Italian manufacturer's adventure in Superbike soon came to an end due to a lack of budget.

Colin Edwards

1° C. EDWARDS	USA	HONDA	400
2° N. HAGA	JPN	YAMAHA	335
3° T. CORSER	AUS	APRILIA	310
4° P.F. CHILI	ITA	SUZUKI	258
5° A. YANAGAWA	JPN	KAWASAKI	247
6° T. BAYLISS	AUS	DUCATI	143
7° B. BOSTROM	USA	DUCATI	174
8° A. SLIGHT	NZE	HONDA	153
9° K. FUJIWARA	JPN	SUZUKI	151
10° G. LAVILLA	ESP	KAWASAKI	133

Noriyuki Haga

Troy Corser

Colin Edwards

Troy Bayliss

2001

The next season found a new idol in Troy Bayliss who thrilled and conquered the fans on a superbly competitive Ducati 998. His chief rival was Colin Edwards, who finished ahead of another factory Ducati rider, American Ben Bostrom. The Californian scored the same number of wins as Bayliss (six) but had to settle for third place.

Corser was unable to improve with the Aprilia, and could only win two races. British rider Neil Hodgson was a constant thorn in the side of the Italian manufacturer with a private Ducati, but the twin-cylinder machines dominated the grid and the results, and only the crumbs were left for Edwards, Corser, Chili, Yanagawa and Laconi.

Benelli entered World Superbike for the first time, but with scarce results.

1° T. BAYLISS	AUS	DUCATI	369
2° C. EDWARDS	USA	HONDA	333
3° B. BOSTROM	USA	DUCATI	312
4° T. CORSER	AUS	APRILIA	284
5° N. HODGSON	GBR	DUCATI	269
6° R. XAUS	ESP	DUCATI	236
7° P.F. CHILI	ITA	SUZUKI	232
8° T. OKADA	JPN	HONDA	176
9° A. YANAGAWA	JPN	KAWASAKI	170
10° G. LAVILLA	ESP	KAWASAKI	166

Colin Edwards

Ben Bostrom

2002

The duel between Bayliss and Edwards again characterised the World Superbike season, which offered an amazing spectacle and which only concluded with an exciting race at the Imola finale. The battle between the two (with Xaus as the interloper) at the Enzo & Dino Ferrari Circuit will remain etched in the memory for ever. Just 11 points separated Edwards and Bayliss at the flag, and then both riders bade farewell to Superbike to make the switch to MotoGP.

The season was utterly dominated by

these two, and the only other win in 26 races went to Tamada at Sugo). Third place went to Neil Hodgson who was then signed up by Ducati for the factory team the following year, while a lot had been expected of Ben Bostrom but the American had a disappointing season. Haga could only score a pole and a fourth place finish for Aprilia in a disappointing season, while the Benelli struggled in the hands of Peter Goddard.

1° C. EDWARDS	USA	HONDA	552
2° T. BAYLISS	AUS	DUCATI	541
3° N. HODGSON	GBR	DUCATI	326
4° N. HAGA	JPN	APRILIA	278
5° B. BOSTROM	USA	DUCATI	261
6° R. XAUS	ESP	DUCATI	249
7° J. TOSELAND	GBR	DUCATI	195
8° P.F. CHILI	ITA	DUCATI	167
9° C. WALKER	GBR	KAWASAKI	152
10° G. LAVILLA	ESP	SUZUKI	130

Troy Bayliss

Colin Edwards

Neil Hodgson

Neil Hodgson

2003

Hodgson repaid the faith in him by taking the title from his hard-charging Spanish team-mate Ruben Xaus. Third place went to the young British rider James Toseland, who was rapidly emerging as a force to contend with in Superbike and who won race 2 at Oschersleben.

Frenchman Régis Laconi finished fourth on another Ducati, the championship now having been turned into a one-make affair following the retirement of nearly all the Jap-

anese factory teams. The first non-Ducati rider was Spain's Gregorio Lavilla who scored seven podiums but failed to win a race. Brands Hatch was notable for a double win by BSB regular Shane Byrne. The three-cylinder Petronas from Malaysia meanwhile made its championship debut in the hands of Troy Corser and James Haydon, but without obtaining any significant results.

1° N. HODGSON	GBR	DUCATI	489
2° R. XAUS	ESP	DUCATI	386
3° J. TOSELAND	GBR	DUCATI	271
4° R. LACONI	FRA	DUCATI	267
5° G. LAVILLA	ESP	SUZUKI	256
6° C. WALKER	GBR	DUCATI	234
7° P.F. CHILI	ITA	DUCATI	197
8° S. MARTIN	AUS	DUCATI	139
9° L. PEDERCINI	ITA	DUCATI	112
10° M. BORCIANI	ITA	DUCATI	111

Ruben Xaus

Neil Hodgson

James Toseland

2004

James Toseland became the youngest-ever World Superbike champion at the age of 23 by defeating Régis Laconi - his team-mate, chief rival and favourite for victory – in the final round of the championship.

The other championship challengers in an exciting season were Noriyuki Haga on a private Ducati 999, who could quite easily have taken the crown had it not been for a series of errors, and the talented youngster from Australia, Chris Vermeulen, who won four races. 'Veteran' Pierfrancesco Chili also had a few good races on an elderly 998 machine, while the Petronas FP1 (called Foggy Petronas in honour of team manager Carl Fogarty) set a couple of pole positions in the hands of Corser.

James Toseland

1° J. TOSELAND	GBR	DUCATI	336
2° R. LACONI	FRA	DUCATI	327
3° N. HAGA	JPN	DUCATI	299
4° C. VERMEULEN	AUS	HONDA	282
5° P.F. CHILI	ITA	DUCATI	243
6° G. MCCOY	AUS	DUCATI	199
7° S. MARTIN	AUS	DUCATI	181
8° L. HASLAM	GBR	DUCATI	169
9° T. CORSER	AUS	PETRONAS	146
10° M. BORCIANI	ITA	DUCATI	130

Regis Laconi

Chris Vermeulen

Noriyuki Haga

Troy Corser

2005

Ducati's winning streak was interrupted in 2005 with a splendid victory for Troy Corser on the four-cylinder Suzuki. The Australian got the better of his fellow-countryman Chris Vermeulen, who took the new Honda close to the title in the first season with new regulations that unified engine size to 1000 cc for all machines.

Corser won eight races and Vermeulen six, leaving little for the rest. The championship again offered a balanced spectacle thanks to the new regulations and the wins were shared between Suzuki, Honda and Ducati; Yamaha won twice with Haga, who finished third overall, ahead of Toseland (Ducati) and Kagayama (Suzuki), who won one race each. The young Italian Lorenzo Lanzi also scored two wins on a factory Ducati.

1° T. CORSER	AUS	**SUZUKI**	433
2° C. VERMEULEN	AUS	**HONDA**	379
3° N. HAGA	JPN	**YAMAHA**	271
4° J. TOSELAND	GBR	**DUCATI**	254
5° Y. KAGAYAMA	JPN	**SUZUKI**	252
6° R. LACONI	FRA	**DUCATI**	221
7° C. WALKER	GBR	**KAWASAKI**	160
8° A. PITT	AUS	**YAMAHA**	156
9° L. LANZI	ITA	**DUCATI**	150
10° P.F. CHILI	ITA	**HONDA**	131

Noriyuki Haga

Chris Vermeulen

2006

Troy Bayliss returned to Superbike after three years in MotoGP and the Australian dominated the season, winning 12 of the 24 races. The Ducati rider got the better of Toseland who after moving to Honda won the opening round in Losail (Qatar).

World champion Corser failed to repeat his previous year's form and could only win two races, while team-mate Kagayama won three. The Australian finished fourth overall, behind Haga who won only one race on a Yamaha at Brands Hatch but who was always in superb form.

Chris Walker gave Kawasaki its only win when he triumphed in the rain at Assen, while Petronas's experience in World Superbike came to a sad end.

Troy Bayliss

1° T. BAYLISS	AUS	DUCATI	431
2° J. TOSELAND	GBR	HONDA	336
3° N. HAGA	JPN	YAMAHA	326
4° T. CORSER	AUS	SUZUKI	254
5° A. PITT	AUS	YAMAHA	250
6° A. BARROS	BRA	HONDA	246
7° Y. KAGAYAMA	JPN	SUZUKI	211
8° L. LANZI	ITA	DUCATI	169
9° C. WALKER	AUS	KAWASAKI	158
10° F. NIETO	SPA	KAWASAKI	139

James Toseland

Toseland and Bayliss

WORLD TITLE VICTORIES (RIDERS)	
Carl FOGARTY	4 (1994 – 1995 1998 – 1999)
Fred MERKEL	2 (1988 – 1989)
Doug POLEN	2 (1991 – 1992)
Troy CORSER	2 (1996 – 2005)
Colin EDWARDS	2 (2000 – 2002)
Troy BAYLISS	2 (2001 – 2006)
James TOSELAND	2 (2004 – 2007)
Raymond ROCHE	1 (1990)
Scott RUSSELL	1 (1993)
John KOCINSKI	1 (1997)
Neil HODGSON	1 (2003)

The best

**Anniversaries are a good opportu-
nity to draw up a balance of activities**
and draw up new ideas and information.

In the next few pages we highlight the
records that belong to some of the riders
and bikes that have made Superbike what it
is today, some of which are simply curious,
others interesting on a technical and sporting level.

ALL-TIME RACE WINNERS	
Carl FOGARTY	59
Troy BAYLISS	41
Troy CORSER	33
Colin EDWARDS	31
Doug POLEN	27
Noriyuki HAGA	26
Raymond ROCHE	23
Piefrancesco CHILI	17
Giancarlo FALAPPA	16
Neil HODGSON	16
James TOSELAND	16

ALL-TIME POLE POSITION WINNERS	
Troy CORSER	40
Carl FOGARTY	21
Troy BAYLISS	18
Doug POLEN	17
Neil HODGSON	16
Colin EDWARDS	15
Piefrancesco CHILI	10
Raymond ROCHE	9
Giancarlo FALAPPA	8
Scott RUSSELL	8
Aaron SLIGHT	8

ALL-TIME POINTS CLASSIFICATION (RIDERS)	
Troy CORSER	3.480,5
Carl FOGARTY	3.020
Aaron SLIGHT	2.834,5
Piefrancesco CHILI	2.788,5
Noriyuki HAGA	2.605
Colin EDWARDS	2.393.5
Troy BAYLISS	2.207
James TOSELAND	2.027
Fabrizio PIROVANO	1.678,5
Neil HODGSON	1.566,5

DOUBLE RACE WINNERS	
Carl FOGARTY	16
Troy BAYLISS	16
Troy CORSER	8
Colin EDWARDS	8
Doug POLEN	8

The best

ALL-TIME RACE PARTICIPATION	
Piefrancesco CHILI	278
Troy CORSER	275
Aaron SLIGHT	229
Carl FOGARTY	219
Noriyuki HAGA	204
Piergiorgio BONTEMPI	195
Fabrizio PIROVANO	183
Lucio PEDERCINI	176
Colin EDWARDS	175
James TOSELAND	168

WORLD TITLE VICTORIES (MANUFACTURERS)		
DUCATI	14	(1991 – 1992
		1993 – 1994
		1995 – 1996
		1998 – 1999
		2000 – 2001
		2002 – 2003
		2004 – 2006)
HONDA	4	(1988 – 1989
		1990 – 1997)
SUZUKI	1	(2005)
YAMAHA	1	(2007)

ALL-TIME MANUFACTURER RACE VICTORIES	
DUCATI	261
HONDA	98
YAMAHA	44
KAWASAKI	35
SUZUKI	25

ALL-TIME POINTS CLASSIFICATION (MANUFACTURERS)	
DUCATI	p. 24.021,5
HONDA	p. 11.669,5
YAMAHA	p. 10.106
KAWASAKI	p. 10.010
SUZUKI	p. 5.262